Because It's My Body!

Library of Congress Cataloging-in-Publication Data
Sherman, Joanne.
Because It's My Body! / by Joanne Sherman;
illustrated by John Steven Gurney
LCCN 2001 129047   ISBN 09711735-9-1
                      ISBN13: 978-0-9711735-9-0

Summary: A series of vignettes teaches children how to assertively
communicate that they do not want to be touched.
1. Child molesting – Prevention – Psychological aspects – Juvenile literature.
2. Privacy – Juvenile literature.
3. Body, Human – Juvenile literature.
4. Touch – Juvenile literature.

10 9 8 7 6 5 4 3 2 1
Text and illustrations © 2002 by Joanne S. Goldstein
Published in 2002 by S.A.F.E. for Children Publishing, L.L.C.,
1814 E. Second Street, Scotch Plains, New Jersey 07076

Printed in the U.S.A.

KEEP 'EM SAFE SERIES:
ANXIETY-FREE LEARNING FOR CHILDREN

Because It's My Body!

BY JOANNE SHERMAN, MS, RN, APN, C
ILLUSTRATED BY JOHN STEVEN GURNEY

S.A.F.E. FOR CHILDREN PUBLISHING ~ NEW JERSEY
SERIOUS ANXIETY-FREE EDUCATION

For my parents,
   who always wanted the best for me.

For my children,
   for whom I will always want the best.

For my husband,
   who brings out the best in me.

Special thanks to all of my family and friends
whose years of love and support
have made all of my accomplishments possible.

Hi! My name is Lindsay.

These are my friends, Todd, Kim, Max and Danny.

We're little kids like you!

It's fun being little.

You get to get tickled,

and you're given rides.

You get lots of hugs,

and kisses!

You get picked up,

and people play all kinds
of funny games with you!!

Sometimes you don't feel like
doing any of those things.

Sometimes you just don't feel like playing with
anybody. It can be hard to get out of playing
with people. Especially big people.

But we know what to do!!

When my babysitter starts to tickle me,
and I don't feel like being tickled, I just say

"No tickling right now, please."

If she asks why not, I say, "I don't feel like laughing."

And if she asks why not again, I say loud and clear,

"Because it's my body!!"

When my favorite uncle comes over and wants to give me his super duper, hold onto your hat and ride 'em cowboy, piggyback ride, and I'm just not into it, I say, "Thanks, partner, not just now."

If he asks why not,
I say, "I've got a hankerin' to do other things."

If he says, "Aw, come on, little cowboy,"

I just say, "No, because it's my body,
and I don't feel like a ride right now!"

When my grandma's best friend stops by to visit,

the one who hugs and squeezes me
the way I squeeze my teddy when I'm scared,

I offer her a high five!

If she tries to put her arms around me, I stand back and say, "Sorry, I'm all hugged out for now!" If she asks how come, I look her right in the eye and say,

"Because it's my body, and I know
I don't feel like being hugged right now!"

Sometimes I'm the patient when my best friend and I play doctor. When she wants to look in my mouth and I don't feel like opening up,

I say, "Doctor, I'm here for a sore thumb."

If she says I have to open my mouth because she's the doctor, I say, "You're not my real doctor, we're only playing. I know what has to be looked at

because it's my body!"

And when someone wants to kiss me, even my mom
or dad, and I don't feel like being kissed, I just say,
"I'm currently not accepting any kisses.
Please check back later!!"

Most times they just say okay, but if they ask why
not, I say, "I don't feel like kisses right now." And
if they ask again why they can't kiss me, I say,

"Because it's my body and
I don't feel like being kissed!!"

Some people love us, and you, so much
that they just can't keep their hands off of us!
We have to remind them what's not okay,

and what is okay with us!!

Sometimes you feel like a hug, or a kiss,

or a piggyback ride,

and sometimes you don't!

It can be hard to think of just what to say.

But we always remember one
very important thing.

Whenever we don't want to be touched,
or hugged, or tickled or kissed,
and someone asks, "Why not?",

it's enough just to say,

Because It's My Body!

143

NOTE TO PARENTS

News media stories of physical and sexual abuse of children have become painfully commonplace. Statistics vary by study, but some claim that as many as 25% of girls and 17% of boys are molested or abused by the time they reach adulthood. Staggering numbers such as these have heightened the sense of urgency for parents, educators, medical and mental health professionals to teach children how to protect themselves. Unfortunately, the way information is imparted to children is not always age appropriate. Thus, what is intended to protect, may unnecessarily and excessively alarm children, as well as potentially emotionally hinder them.

The most commonly used phrase in this teaching process which raises concern is "private parts." This choice of words too strongly suggests to children (and adults) that sexual anatomy is never to be viewed or touched. Early and prolonged education of young children with these kinds of sentiments (including 'bathing suit area,' etc.) runs a risk of distorting healthy sexuality in adult life. The message we want to convey, rather, is that *INAPPROPRIATE* viewing and touching is unacceptable.

The express purpose of this book is to help parents to empower their children to be able to declare what they deem as appropriate and inappropriate (i.e. acceptable and unacceptable) touching or viewing of their bodies at any given moment in time. The message to the children is that they have exclusive rights over their entire bodies. This communication offers children a substantially healthier and more positive attitude upon which to grow. A child who learns at home that it is permissible to say "No!" to being touched, even casually by family members and friends is decidedly more apt and capable of saying no to inappropriate touching/viewing initiated by other adults or children. It is important to note that the vast number of perpetrators against children are people that the children know and trust. It is equally important to know that convicted pedophiles frequently acknowledge that they preyed upon children who would not resist their advances. Saying "No!" can be a powerful form of resistance in the face of a perpetrator who does not want to raise suspicion or call attention to themselves.

This book teaches a kind of assertiveness which raises anxiety for many parents. Parents fear that their child will be viewed as rude for refusing to kiss or hug, or be kissed or hugged by extended family and close friends. A twofold response: First, polite behavior in greeting or saying good-bye need not necessarily include touching. A child who is taught how to articulate a gracious greeting and farewell will assuredly be well received, even by those who had hoped for a kiss. Secondly, parents who literally stand beside their children and verbally give them permission to use words rather than touch when they have been beckoned by another are helping their children to grow into their independence. It is very hard for children to stand up to adults and not deliver what is asked of them (e.g. kiss, hug). It is up to parents to teach their children that respectful behavior is not the same as unchallenged submissiveness.

Permitting your children to reject your own advances of physical affection may be the single greatest lesson you can teach and gift you can give with regard to preventing sexual molestation. Every time you respect their wish to not be touched, you are reinforcing their sense of themselves and therefore, empowering them. Be alert to their gestures which indicate times when they do not want to be touched and as their speech develops, encourage them to use words to say so. Then grant them their space. Children who can say "No" to their parents are best prepared to say "No" to others.

This book offers parents and children a lighthearted look at ways of getting out of "ticklish" situations in which kids often find themselves. Enjoy the silliness of the book, its words and illustrations with your child. Ask your child how else the children on each page could get their messages across. It is important that you read the book aloud as you would any other age appropriate book. There is no need to probe or lecture while reading. It is through your voicing approval and enjoyment of what's happening on each page that the message will be conveyed to your child.